ISBN 0-86163-629-5 (cased)

Text copyright © Christine Butterworth 1990
Illustrations copyright © Barbara Walker 1990

This edition first published 1993 by
Award Publications Limited,
The Old Riding School, Welbeck Estate,
Nr Worksop, Nottinghamshire

First published 1990 by Hodder and Stoughton
Children's Books

Printed in Singapore

BEANS

Christine Butterworth

Illustrated by Barbara Walker

AWARD PUBLICATIONS LIMITED

Lou helps her dad to pick
runner beans which grow in
their garden. She has to stand
on tiptoe to reach the long ones
which grow high up.

Lou cuts open the green runner
bean pod to find the shiny
purple beans inside. She slices
the pod for her mum to boil in
water for dinner.

Each year Lou's dad keeps
some of the purple beans until
they go hard and dry. These
are the seeds he will plant next
spring to grow into more
runner bean plants.

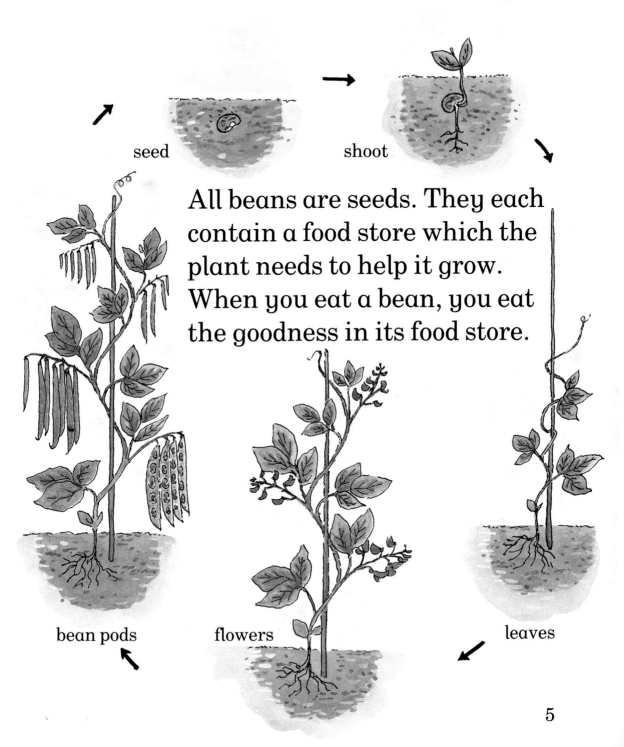

seed

shoot

All beans are seeds. They each
contain a food store which the
plant needs to help it grow.
When you eat a bean, you eat
the goodness in its food store.

bean pods

flowers

leaves

5

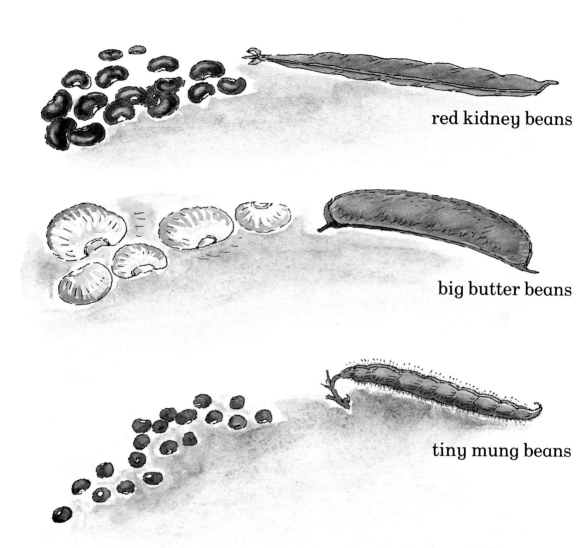

red kidney beans

big butter beans

tiny mung beans

All kinds of beans have the sort
of goodness found in meat and
vegetables.

Lou's mum has lots of dried beans in jars on her kitchen shelf. Lou loves all the different colours. She glues beans onto paper to make a picture.

Dried beans keep for a long
time, but they are very hard.
You have to soak them in
water for hours before you
can cook them.

Some beans must not be kept
for too long, or they will go
stale. Peanuts are beans like
this. Peanut plants grow in
North America, Africa, India
and China.

Peanut pods grow underground,
or round the base of the plant.

The pods are dug up, cleaned
and dried. The nuts are shelled
and roasted.

Peanut butter is made by
grinding peanuts into powder,
and mixing the powder with oil
and salt. Do you like peanut
butter which is smooth or
crunchy?

Beans are eaten all over the
world. They are an important
food for families who live in a
country where food may be
scarce.

The little soya bean is the most
useful bean because it can be
made into so many different
foods.

barbecued
spare ribs

pork and
green
peppers

In China and Japan they make
soya milk, soya flour, and bean
curd from soya beans. They also
make salty brown soy sauce to
add flavour to their food.

spicy chicken

Soya beans have lots of oil in them. When the beans are crushed, the oil is used to make margarine and cooking oil.

bean sprouts

prawns

stir fry beef and mushrooms

15

Lou grows tiny mung beans
into bean sprouts to eat in a
salad. She washes them

puts them in a jar

and covers the jar with muslin.

She keeps them in a warm
place and rinses them twice a
day with cold water.

In about four days the sprouts
grow. Lou eats them when they
are about 2 cms long.

Even chocolate is made from beans. Cocoa bean trees grow in Brazil and Africa. Big pods grow out of the tree trunk. The pods are cut open to get the beans out.

The beans are piled up and left
for six days. This is when they
get their chocolate taste.

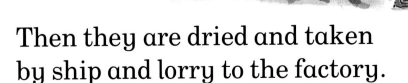

Then they are dried and taken
by ship and lorry to the factory.

The beans are roasted and
ground into a thick paste. Some
of this is made into cocoa. The
rest is made into chocolate.

Lou's favourite beans are
baked beans. These start as
small white haricot beans.
Each raw bean is checked in
the factory by a 'magic eye' to
find any bad beans.

The beans are partly cooked
before they are put into cans.
The cans are filled with tomato
sauce, sealed and cooked until
the beans are done.

'This kitchen is just like me,'
says Lou. 'It's full of beans!'

How many kinds of beans are
there in your kitchen?

bean words

baked beans

bean pods

bean sprouts

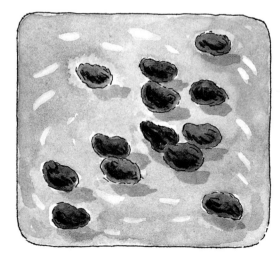

cocoa beans

dried beans

soya beans

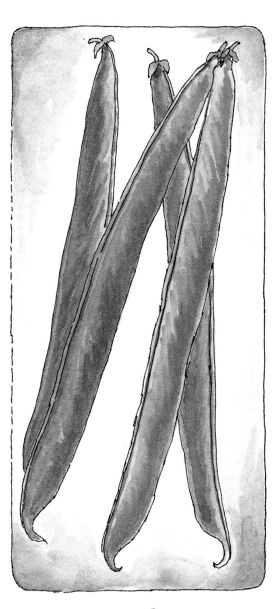

runner beans

25